Math Matters!

Adding

Look out for these sections to help you learn more about each topic:

Remember…

This provides a summary of the key concept(s) on each two-page entry. Use it to revise what you have learned.

Word check

These are new and important words that help you understand the ideas presented on each two-page entry.

All of the word check entries in this book are shown in the glossary on page 45. The versions in the glossary are sometimes more extensive explanations.

Book link…

Although this book can be used on its own, other titles in the *Math Matters!* set may provide more information on certain topics. This section tells you which other titles to refer to.

Place value ·

To make it easy for you to see exactly what we are doing, you will find colored columns behind the numbers in all the examples on this and the following pages. This is what the colors mean:

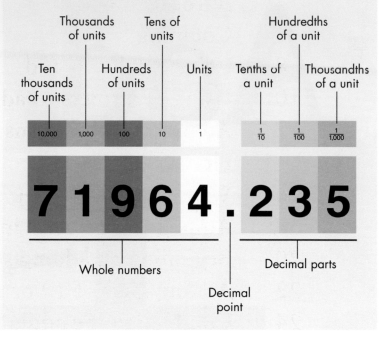

71964.235

Ten thousands of units — 10,000
Thousands of units — 1,000
Hundreds of units — 100
Tens of units — 10
Units — 1
Tenths of a unit — $\frac{1}{10}$
Hundredths of a unit — $\frac{1}{100}$
Thousandths of a unit — $\frac{1}{1,000}$

Whole numbers

Decimal point

Decimal parts

Series concept by *Brian Knapp and Duncan McCrae*
Text contributed by *Brian Knapp and Colin Bass*
Design and production by *Duncan McCrae*
Illustrations of characters by *Nicolas Debon*
Digital illustrations by *David Woodroffe*
Other illustrations by *Peter Bull Art Studio*
Editing by *Lorna Gilbert and Barbara Carragher*
Layout by *Duncan McCrae and Mark Palmer*
Reprographics by *Global Colour*
Printed and bound by *LEGO SpA*

First Published in the United States in 1999 by Grolier Educational, Sherman Turnpike, Danbury, CT 06816

Copyright © 1999
Atlantic Europe Publishing Company Limited

Library of Congress Cataloging-in-Publication Data
Math Matters!
    p. cm.
    Includes indexes.
    Contents: v.1.Numbers — v.2.Adding — v.3.Subtracting — v.4.Multiplying — v.5.Dividing — v.6.Decimals — v.7.Fractions – v.8.Shape — v.9.Size — v.10.Tables and Charts — v.11.Grids and Graphs — v.12.Chance and Average — v.13.Mental Arithmetic
ISBN 0–7172–9294–0 (set: alk. paper). — ISBN 0–7172–9295–9 (v.1: alk. paper). — ISBN 0–7172–9296–7 (v.2: alk. paper). — ISBN 0–7172–9297–5 (v.3: alk. paper). — ISBN 0–7172–9298–3 (v.4: alk. paper). — ISBN 0–7172–9299–1 (v.5: alk. paper). — ISBN 0–7172–9300–9 (v.6: alk. paper). — ISBN 0–7172–9301–7 (v.7: alk. paper). — ISBN 0–7172–9302–5 (v.8: alk. paper). — ISBN 0–7172–9303–3 (v.9: alk. paper). — ISBN 0–7172–9304–1 (v.10: alk. paper). — ISBN 0–7172–9305–X (v.11: alk. paper). — ISBN 0–7172–9306–8 (v.12: alk. paper). — ISBN 0–7172–9307–6 (v.13: alk. paper).

    1. Mathematics — Juvenile literature. [1. Mathematics.]
I. Grolier Educational Corporation.
QA40.5.M38   1998
510 — dc21   98–7404
                                                        CIP
                                                        AC

Contents

Introduction

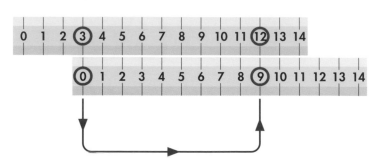

Although we can get by simply by counting one number after another, counting is not adding. Adding is a short-cut way of building bigger numbers quickly and efficiently.

In counting all you do is give each item you are counting a new number, one higher than the last. Adding is far smarter and quicker than counting. But it is even more powerful than this, as you will see.

Adding is a part of arithmetic. It has its own special words, but they are easy to learn. For example, when we add two numbers together, the number we get is called the sum. This is why people sometimes say "they are doing their sums" — they are adding things up.

2 + 7 = 9

$$2 + 7 = 9 \longrightarrow \begin{array}{r} 2 \\ + 7 \\ \hline 9 \end{array}$$

$$\frac{4}{12} + \frac{3}{12} = \frac{7}{12}$$

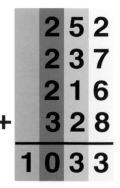

$$\begin{array}{r} 252 \\ 237 \\ 216 \\ + 328 \\ \hline 1033 \end{array}$$

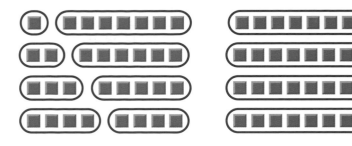

Adding has only a few simple rules. There are also some basic adding facts to learn and some clever tricks that save time and allow you to check your answers.

You will find that by following the simple stages in this book, it will be easy to learn all about adding. Each idea is set out on a separate page, so that you can quickly refer back to an idea if you have forgotten it.

Like all of the books in this mathematics set, there are many examples. They have been designed to be quite varied because you can use mathematics at any time, any place, anywhere. Some of the examples are based on fun stories, so have fun reading them as you go.

$$\begin{array}{r} 9 \\ + 5 \\ \hline 1\,4 \end{array}$$

$$\begin{array}{r} 9\,2 \\ + 4\,6 \\ \hline ?\,3\,8 \end{array}$$
1

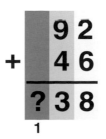

+	0	1	2	3	4	5	6	7	8	9
0	0	1	2	3	4	5	6	7	8	9
1	1	2	3	4	5	6	7	8	9	
2	2	3	4	5	6	7	8	9		
3	3	4	5	6	7	8	9			
4	4	5	6	7	8	9				
5	5	6	7	8	9					
6	6	7	8	9						
7	7	8	9							
8	8	9								
9	9									

Counting

Counting is the simplest thing you can do with numbers. It is just a matter of moving on one number at a time.

A good example of how to count is the way we use calendars. In a calendar all the dates for each month are shown. We use counting to find out such things as how long it is to the end of the school term, or how long it is to a friend's birthday. Here is a common example.

Emily's mother told her that Aunt Emma's birthday would be in five days' time. Emily wanted to know what date that would be. She knew that it was September 16th. So she needed to count from then. Emily used the help of her fingers to count from the 16th:

In one day
it would be the 17th.

In two days
it would be the 18th.

In three days
it would be the 19th.

In four days
it would be the 20th.

And in five days
it would be the 21st.

Counting with long numbers

Counting with your fingers is easy when the number involved is **10** or less. But Emily also knew that it would be her brother's birthday in **23** days' time, and she wanted to find out what the date would be. So was there an easier way to find out than using fingers?

Emily could certainly have used another method that didn't need fingers if she'd had a calendar handy. She could have counted on using the dates printed on the calendar.

By counting using the calendar, you can see that her brother's birthday is on Thursday, October 9th.

Tip... People who use counting a lot often count not just one at a time but two at a time. For example, people in warehouses often have to count up the number of items they have on the shelves. So they count 2, 4, 6, 8...

Counting in twos can cut their counting time in half!

SEPTEMBER

SUN	MON	TUE	WED	THU	FRI	SAT
	1	2	3	4	5	6
7	8	9	10	11	12	13
14	15	16	17	18	19	20
21	22	23	24	25	26	27
28	29	30				

OCTOBER

SUN	MON	TUE	WED	THU	FRI	SAT
			1	2	3	4
5	6	7	8	9	10	11
12	13	14	15	16	17	18
19	20	21	22	23	24	25
26	27	28	29	30		

Remember... In counting you work through the numbers one at a time. You can count up or down.

Word check

Counting: Finding the result in a set of things by giving each item a number one more than the last one used.

Using a ruler to add

The idea of counting is at the heart of adding. When we are adding, we are always asking, "What is the answer when we add (count from) one number to another?" To make this easy, we can use a simple number line, such as the ruler marked off in whole numbers shown below.

Jackie has a collection of **4** books. She buys (adds) **5** more. How many has she got now?

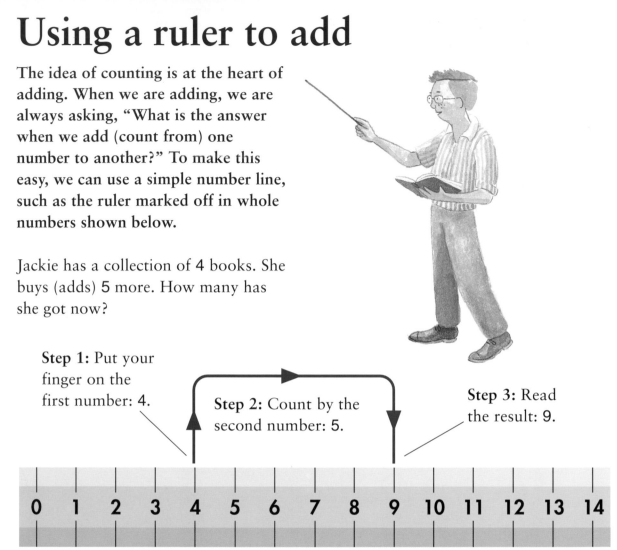

Step 1: Put your finger on the first number: 4.

Step 2: Count by the second number: 5.

Step 3: Read the result: 9.

A ruler used as a number line for counting

One way of showing what we have done is to use words, for example:

Four and five makes nine

Or as a word equation:

Four plus five equals nine

And as a number equation this is:

$$4 + 5 = 9$$

Joaquin phoned up his local record store to find out how long he would have to wait for the new CD going on sale that day. He was told about **23** minutes. When he arrived at the shop, he found that lots more people had recently joined the line, and the wait had gone up by **8** minutes more than he was told on the phone. How long would Joaquin have to wait?

Book link... You can find out more about using this ruler for subtracting in the book *Subtracting* in the *Math Matters!* set.

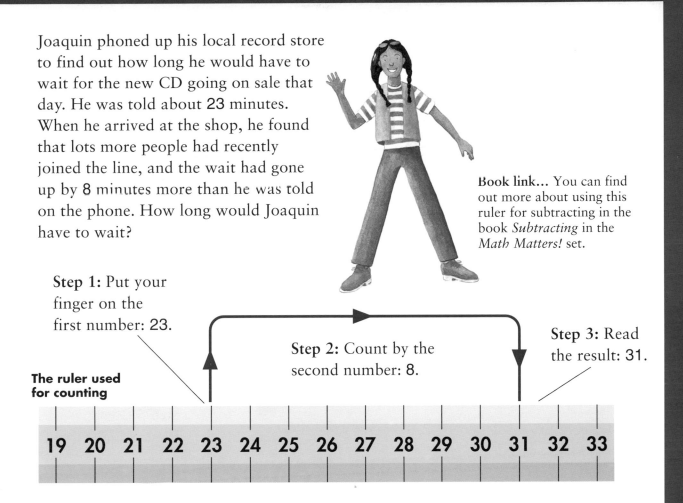

Step 1: Put your finger on the first number: 23.

Step 2: Count by the second number: 8.

Step 3: Read the result: 31.

The ruler used for counting

| 19 | 20 | 21 | 22 | 23 | 24 | 25 | 26 | 27 | 28 | 29 | 30 | 31 | 32 | 33 |

Joaquin had to wait for **31** minutes

We can write what we have done as:

Twenty-three plus eight makes thirty-one

Which as a number equation is:

$$23 + 8 = 31$$

Remember... To add using a ruler, put your finger on the first number, count along the ruler by the second number, and read off the result.

Word check

+ : The symbol for adding. We say it "plus."

= : The symbol for equals. We say it "equals" or "makes."

Adding: A quick way of counting.

Equation: A number sentence using the = symbol, telling us that two different ways of writing a number are the same. For example, $2 + 2 = 4$ and $9 - 5 = 4$.

Using two rulers to add

To speed up your counting, you can use two rulers side by side. This will make an adding slide rule to help you with simple adding problems.

Problem

To add 3 and 9 by sliding rulers.

$$3 + 9 = ?$$

Step 1: Put the zero of ruler B against the first number to be added on ruler A. In this case it is 3.

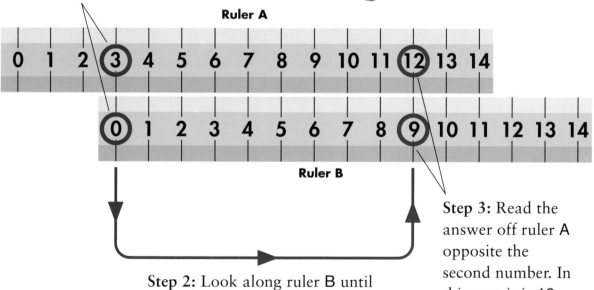

Ruler A

Ruler B

Step 2: Look along ruler B until you come to the second number to be added. In this case it is 9.

Step 3: Read the answer off ruler A opposite the second number. In this case it is 12.

From the rulers we can therefore work out that:

$$3 + 9 = 12$$

Problem

To add 12 and 15 using two rulers.

$$12 + 15 = ?$$

Step 1: Put the zero of ruler B against the first number to be added on ruler A. In this case it is 12.

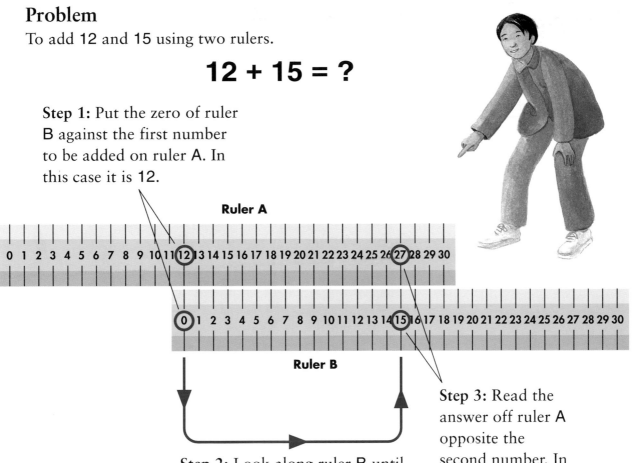

Ruler A

Ruler B

Step 2: Look along ruler B until you come to the second number to be added. In this case it is 15.

Step 3: Read the answer off ruler A opposite the second number. In this case it is 27.

Therefore the sum of twelve and fifteen is twenty-seven:

$$12 + 15 = 27$$

Remember… To add with two rulers, you place the zero of one ruler against the first number you want to add on the other ruler. Then look along the second ruler until you find the next number. Read the answer off the first ruler.

Word check

Sum: The result of adding two or more numbers. Another word for sum is total.

Also… You will see that the pair of rulers makes adding quite fast, and you don't even have to know how to add! But it does have problems: as you can see, you soon run out of numbers because your ruler is usually quite short! This is why it is so useful to learn about adding, as we will do on the next page…

Adding using patterns

We find it very slow and difficult to count large quantities of things. Arranging them in patterns can make it easier for us to add them.

Let's look at an example. The nest on the right contains eggs. But can you see how many of them there are at a glance?

You probably found this difficult because most of us find it difficult to recognize a group of more than five objects at a glance. After that the brain needs some help, and we have to start counting!

The importance of patterns

Just think about the way you worked out how many eggs there were in the picture above. You had to count the eggs one at a time. Now look at the eggs in the box on the right.

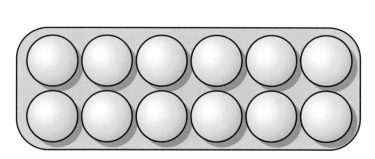

Did you count every egg to find out how many there were? Or did you count along one row to get 6 and then say to yourself: "There are two rows of 6, and so there are 12 eggs in the box."

Your brain added two counting numbers together. We would say this as:

6 eggs and 6 eggs makes 12 eggs

And using symbols, it is:

6 + 6 = 12

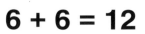

Working fast with patterns

Your brain works faster with patterns.
This is the reason playing cards have their
markings arranged in patterns.

Notice that by using patterns, you can easily
recognize a card with a value of 8, 9, or 10:

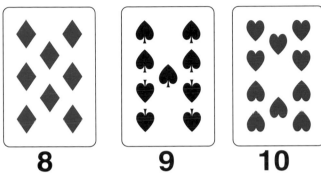

But how did your brain do this? Well, it
probably looked at the patterns, counted the
marks in one pattern, noticed there was more
than one similar pattern, and <u>put together</u>, or
<u>added</u>, the number in each pattern.

For example, a "ten" card has 2 patterns of 5
marks. You might say to yourself, "5 and 5
hearts makes 10 hearts."

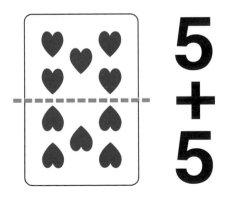

Using symbols, it is: **5 + 5 = 10**

Remember… Thinking in terms of patterns
can speed up your work. Easy patterns
include 2's, 5's, and 10's.

First adding facts

How can you easily count a total of eight pieces of chocolate? To find out, you can arrange them into groups. At the same time, you will produce a collection of important adding facts.

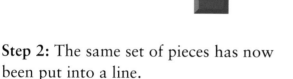

This is the shape used for a single chocolate piece. It can also be called a <u>unit</u>.

Step 1: These are the chocolate pieces laid out with no pattern.

Step 2: The same set of pieces has now been put into a line.

Step 3: The pieces have now been arranged into groups. The numbers tell you how many are in each group. There are always eight pieces in each line in this example:

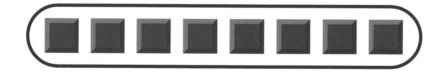

Line 1   **1** + **7** = **8**

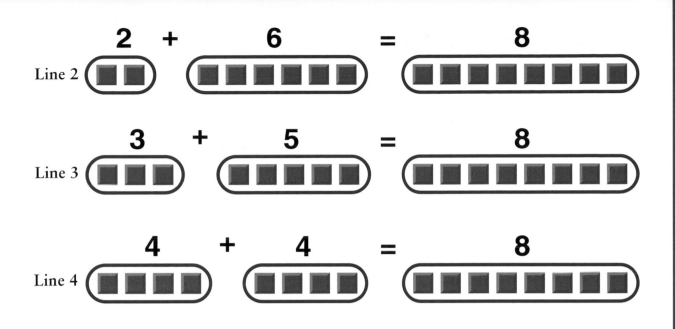

2 + 6 = 8

Line 2

3 + 5 = 8

Line 3

4 + 4 = 8

Line 4

Notice that we have shown the mathematical symbols above each line.

Line 1 is: **1 + 7 = 8**

Line 2 is: **2 + 6 = 8**

Line 3 is: **3 + 5 = 8**

Line 4 is: **4 + 4 = 8**

Each of these additions is called an <u>adding fact</u>. We will find many more as we go along.

Remember… You can get more simple adding facts by adding any numbers you choose. You may want to use your adding rulers.

Word check

Adding facts: The numbers produced by adding together numbers that we use a lot, such as 3 + 4 = 7. These are facts we remember rather than work out each time.

Unit: 1 of something. A small square shape representing 1.

Using columns to add

Numbers are most easily added by placing them in columns.

It is always best to try to find simple, easily understood ways of writing things down. Here is how we write down a sum of two single numbers, also called single digits.

First, we have to plan ahead. Later in the book we will be adding together some very big numbers. But putting large numbers in rows makes adding very difficult. So we put them in columns instead.

The key idea is to make sure the numbers are exactly one above the other in the columns. We will guide you in this book by using colored columns. In this case the yellow color of the column also tells you that the numbers are all units (see page 2 for more help with colored columns).

This yellow-colored column is used to make sure that all the numbers stay exactly one above each other. You will see how important this is when we add large numbers together.

This is the sum set out in a column.

For example, we can put 3 + 4 = 7 into columns like this:

This is the equation written out in a row.

$$3 + 4 = 7$$

Units

$$3$$
$$+$$
$$4$$
$$=$$
$$7$$

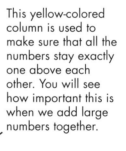

Units

$$3$$
$$+$$
$$4$$
$$\overline{7}$$

Units

$$3$$
$$+ \, 4$$
$$\overline{7}$$

When adding is done in columns, the = sign is replaced by a single line.

Here are three more simple examples to help
you see how adding columns works.

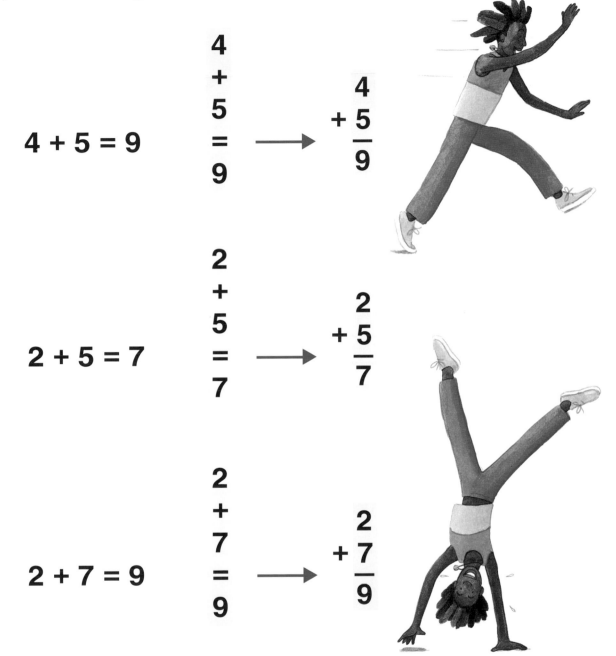

$4 + 5 = 9$

$$\begin{array}{r} 4 \\ + 5 \\ \hline 9 \end{array}$$

$$\begin{array}{r} 4 \\ + 5 \\ \hline 9 \end{array}$$

$2 + 5 = 7$

$$\begin{array}{r} 2 \\ + 5 \\ \hline 7 \end{array}$$

$$\begin{array}{r} 2 \\ + 5 \\ \hline 7 \end{array}$$

$2 + 7 = 9$

$$\begin{array}{r} 2 \\ + 7 \\ \hline 9 \end{array}$$

$$\begin{array}{r} 2 \\ + 7 \\ \hline 9 \end{array}$$

Remember... You place numbers in
columns for adding. You don't have to
draw in the columns, but you should
always write out your work in columns.

Word check
Digit: The numerals 1, 2, 3, 4, 5, 6,
7, 8, 9, or 0. Several may be used to
stand for a larger number.

Adding can be done in any order

We can take a group of things and separate them in different ways, but the total number of things remains the same, no matter how we split them up.

For example, if we take a group of seven things, we can split them into different groups like this. They always add up to 7.

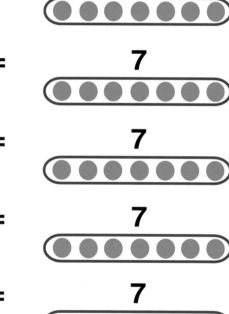

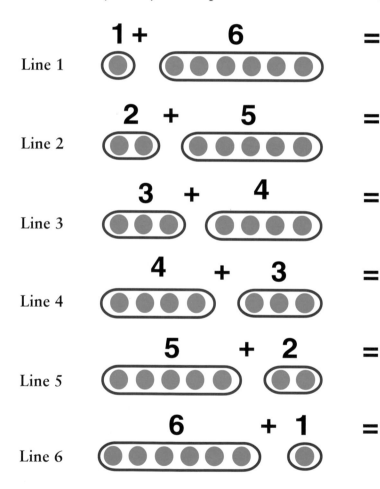

Line 1   **1 +   6   =   7**

Line 2   **2 +   5   =   7**

Line 3   **3 +   4   =   7**

Line 4   **4 +   3   =   7**

Line 5   **5 +   2   =   7**

Line 6   **6 + 1   =   7**

Here you can also see one of the important facts to learn about adding: whatever order the numbers are added in, they still make the same total.

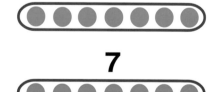

This means that it doesn't matter which order you add, the total will always be the same. This is called the "Turn-Around Rule": you can turn the numbers around as much as you want in adding, the sum will always be the same.

For example, in line 1 on the opposite page you have a group of 1 and a group of 6.

$$1 + 6 = 7$$

On line 6 you will see that the things have been arranged so that there is a group of 6 and a group of 1. But the total is still 7.

$$6 + 1 = 7$$

You will find the same patterns in each of the other combinations of groups in the pattern.

Lines 3 and 4

$$3 + 4 = 7 \text{ and } 4 + 3 = 7$$

Lines 2 and 5

$$2 + 5 = 7 \text{ and } 5 + 2 = 7$$

Remember... Adding follows the "Turn-Around Rule." When we add the same two numbers, the answer is the same no matter which of the numbers comes first.

Word check

Turn-Around Rule: When we add or multiply the same two numbers, the answer is the same no matter which of the numbers comes first (but it does not hold for subtracting or dividing).

Also... The fact that numbers can be added in any order remains true for huge numbers as well.

So, $98,047 + 537,165 = 635,212$ and $537,165 + 98,047 = 635,212$. You can check this using your calculator.

Beginning an adding square

Compared with counting, adding saves time in two ways. First, we don't have to go back to the beginning every time. Second, we can learn some simple sums that are always the same, and that we can use over and over again. These are called <u>adding facts</u>.

Adding facts can be placed together in a square to make learning them easier.

Adding facts to 9

It is very important to learn adding facts if we are to do adding well.

There are three steps:

1. Check that the facts we are using are correct.
2. Find a neat way of writing down the facts, so that we don't have to keep checking them.
3. Learn them by heart.

We found out some adding facts on earlier pages. On the right you can see a neat way to write down these adding facts and many others besides.

We first write down each of the numbers between 0 and 9 to make two of the sides of our square.

Then we fill in the sums as you can see on the next page.

+	0	1	2	3	4	5	6	7	8	9
0										
1										
2										
3										
4										
5										
6										
7										
8										
9										

How to use the adding square

Step 1: You choose the first number you want to add from the top row.

Step 2: You choose the other number you want to add from the left column.

Follow down the column from the first number, 5.

Read the answer to the adding sum.

Follow along the row from the second number, 3.

+	0	1	2	3	4	5	6	7	8	9
0	0	1	2	3	4	5	6	7	8	9
1	1	2	3	4	5	6	7	8	9	
2	2	3	4	5	6	7	8	9		
3	3	4	5	6	7	8	9			
4	4	5	6	7	8	9				
5	5	6	7	8	9					
6	6	7	8	9						
7	7	8	9							
8	8	9								
9	9									

See the adding square completed on page 25.

Step 3: You read the answer from where the row and column cross.

Example: To add 5 and 3 using the adding square, follow down from the 5 in the top row and along from 3 in the left column to get to 8 in the square.

5 + 3 = 8

or follow across from 5 in the left column and down from 3 in the top row (the Turn-Around Rule).

Remember... An adding square makes it easier to learn the sum of two small numbers. These are the numbers we use every day.

Word check

Adding facts: The numbers produced by adding together numbers that we use a lot, such as 3 + 4 = 7. These are facts we remember rather than work out each time.

Adding square: Simple adding facts arranged in a square pattern to make it easier to learn them.

Adding facts for 10 or more

Sometimes, when we count up two single-digit numbers (units), such as **4 + 7**, the total comes to **10** or more. But we can only put up to **9** in any one column. If we want to put down more than **9**, we have to carry over the extra amount to the next column on the left. Here is the method for adding these kinds of numbers.

Begin by counting these oranges:

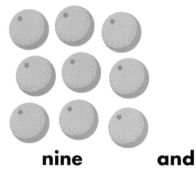 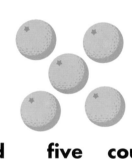 

nine   **and**   **five**   **count up to**   **fourteen**

We can write this as an equation by replacing words with symbols:

$$9 + 5 = 14$$

Similarly:

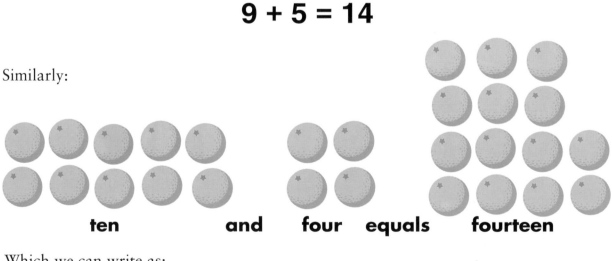

ten   **and**   **four**   **equals**   **fourteen**

Which we can write as:

$$10 + 4 = 14$$

Using columns

The columns hold our numbers. We are using colored columns to remind us that where we place a number is very important.

When we place it on the right (in a yellow-colored column), we are saying its value is only units (1 to 9).

When we place it in the next column to the left (a gold-colored column), we are saying that its value is in the tens (10 to 90).

If there are no units, we hold the place of the units open by putting a 0 in the correct column.

Tens	Units
1	0
+	4
1	4

There is a 1 (one ten) in the tens column and 0 (zero) in the units column. We are adding 4 units, so we put the 4 below the 0. The result is 0 + 4 = 4 in the units column and 1(+ 0) in the tens column, giving the answer 14.

Carrying to the left

We use the same idea for adding 9 + 5 as we did for 10 + 4.

Both 9 and 5 are units, so they go above one another in the units column.

We know from the opposite page that 9 + 5 = 10 + 4, so we put 4 in the units column and carry 1 into the tens column, where we write it down.

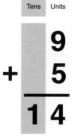

Tens	Units
	9
+	5
1	4

These numbers come to more than 9. Put one of the 5 units with the 9 to make 10, carry it into the next column. Four units are left from the five, and these are written down in the units column.

Remember... We cannot put more than 9 in a column; we have to carry over the extra amount to the next column on the left.

Word check

Carrying: In adding or multiplying, when the working column total is bigger than 10, this is the method of adding the left digit at the bottom of the column on the left.

Single-digit number: A number between 0 and 9.

Completing the adding square

The number facts above **9** that we began to see on page 21 can easily be included in the adding square. They all have a single **1** in the tens column. No number in the square is greater than **18** because 9 + 9 = 18.

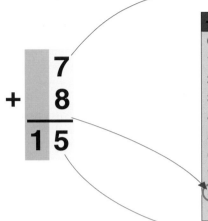

+	0	1	2	3	4	5	6	7	8	9
0	0	1	2	3	4	5	6	7	8	9
1	1	2	3	4	5	6	7	8	9	10
2	2	3	4	5	6	7	8	9	10	11
3	3	4	5	6	7	8	9	10	11	12
4	4	5	6	7	8	9	10	11	12	13
5	5	6	7	8	9	10	11	12	13	14
6	6	7	8	9	10	11	12	13	14	15
7	7	8	9	10	11	12	13	14	15	16
8	8	9	10	11	12	13	14	15	16	17
9	9	10	11	12	13	14	15	16	17	18

Enough sausages?

Fred went to the freezer to get some sausages. His mom wanted at least **16** for their family supper. Fred found that one bag of loose sausages contained **9** sausages, while another contained **8**. He took a small copy of the adding table out of his shirt pocket and read the answer. It was **17**, and so he was able to leave one sausage in the freezer and take out the rest (16 + 1 = 17).

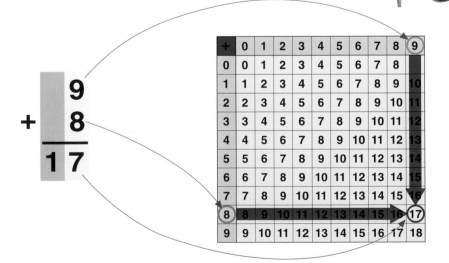

+	0	1	2	3	4	5	6	7	8	9
0	0	1	2	3	4	5	6	7	8	9
1	1	2	3	4	5	6	7	8	9	10
2	2	3	4	5	6	7	8	9	10	11
3	3	4	5	6	7	8	9	10	11	12
4	4	5	6	7	8	9	10	11	12	13
5	5	6	7	8	9	10	11	12	13	14
6	6	7	8	9	10	11	12	13	14	15
7	7	8	9	10	11	12	13	14	15	16
8	8	9	10	11	12	13	14	15	16	17
9	9	10	11	12	13	14	15	16	17	18

Here is a large copy of the adding square so that you can practice looking up more adding facts.

+	0	1	2	3	4	5	6	7	8	9
0	0	1	2	3	4	5	6	7	8	9
1	1	2	3	4	5	6	7	8	9	10
2	2	3	4	5	6	7	8	9	10	11
3	3	4	5	6	7	8	9	10	11	12
4	4	5	6	7	8	9	10	11	12	13
5	5	6	7	8	9	10	11	12	13	14
6	6	7	8	9	10	11	12	13	14	15
7	7	8	9	10	11	12	13	14	15	16
8	8	9	10	11	12	13	14	15	16	17
9	9	10	11	12	13	14	15	16	17	18

Remember... To look for patterns. If you can find patterns in the mathematics you learn, you will find many easy ways to learn facts, and also many short cuts. In this case you will know that although there are 100 adding facts in the square, because numbers can be added in any order, you only have to learn half of them.

Adding using shapes

As numbers get bigger, they can be less easy to work with. Counting gets harder. If you are not sure how to add or are having problems with columns, then one way is to set out the problem as a model using shapes like the ones shown here. You may want to make your own shapes, cut from paper, to work out other problems.

◄ This is a shape for 100. You can prove this by counting up all 100 squares, or units, if you like. Some people call this shape a <u>flat</u>.

◄ This is a shape for 10. Some people call this a <u>long</u>. Ten longs make a flat.

◄ This is a shape for 1. It can also be called a <u>unit</u>. We first met a unit on page 14. 10 units make a long.

Adding **13** and **5** using shapes

13   **+**   **5**

We could simply count along the row. But we can make it easier by replacing ten units with a long, for 10. So 13 becomes 10 + 3.

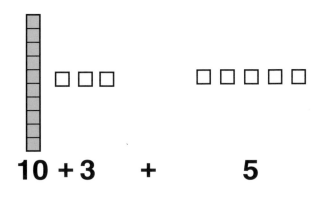

10 + 3   **+**   **5**

So, 13 + 5 is the same as 10 + 3 + 5, which is 10 + 8, which is 18.

Adding **25** and **81** using shapes

We use 2 longs and 5 units for 25 and 8 longs and 1 unit for 81.

25   **+**   **81**

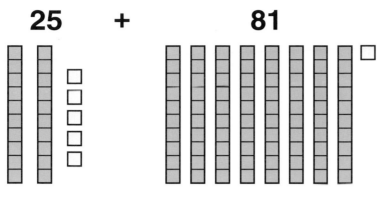

Adding 2 longs and 8 longs gives 10 longs (which is 1 flat, worth 100), and adding 5 units and 1 unit gives us 6 units. So the answer is 106.

=   **100**   **+ 6**   **=**   **106**

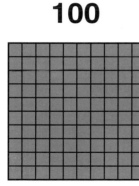

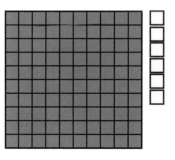

Remember... We can use shapes to help us see what is happening as we add. We know that we can use longs of 10 and flats of 100 to show bigger numbers. But eventually we need to learn to add without shapes!

Word check

Flat: A large square representing 100. It can also be made up of ten "longs" put side by side.

Long: A long shape representing 10.

Unit: A small, square shape representing 1.

Adding numbers between 10 and 99

We have already used columns to help with our adding. On this page you can really see how useful this is. All the numbers on this page contain two-digit numbers (that is, numbers between **10** and **99**), so there is always a number in the tens column as well as a number in the units column. In the last of the examples the answer is in the hundreds. This is a three-digit number that uses three columns.

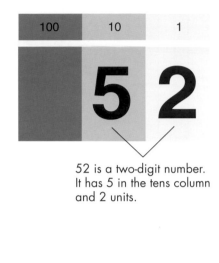

100	10	1

5 2

52 is a two-digit number. It has 5 in the tens column and 2 units.

Here is how to add two two-digit numbers. In this example the answer is also two digits:

52 + 26 = ?

Step 1: Line up the numbers. Put one number below the other in a column, lining the numbers up on the right. Draw a line below them. The answer goes below the line.

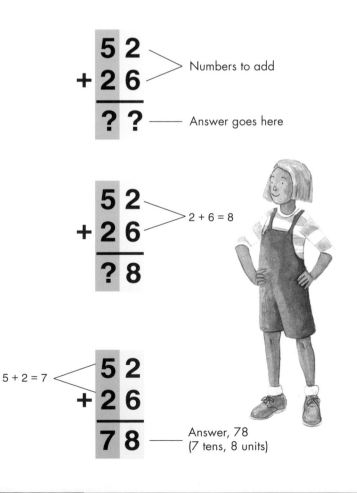

$$\begin{array}{r} 5\,2 \\ +\,2\,6 \\ \hline ?\,? \end{array}$$

Numbers to add

Answer goes here

Step 2: Start with units. Add the right-hand column first. In this case 2 + 6 = 8.

$$\begin{array}{r} 5\,2 \\ +\,2\,6 \\ \hline ?\,8 \end{array}$$

2 + 6 = 8

Step 3: Now add the next column to the left. This is the tens column: 5 + 2 = 7. (Really 50 + 20 = 70)

5 + 2 = 7

$$\begin{array}{r} 5\,2 \\ +\,2\,6 \\ \hline 7\,8 \end{array}$$

Answer, 78 (7 tens, 8 units)

In this example the answer is a three-digit number:

92 + 46 = ?

Step 1: Line up the numbers. Put one number below the other in a column, lining the numbers up on the right.

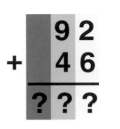

```
  9 2
+ 4 6
-----
? ? ?
```

Step 2: Add the right-hand column first: 2 + 6 = 8.

```
  9 2
+ 4 6
-----
? ? 8
```

These numbers in the units column add to less than 10, and so there is nothing to carry over.

Step 3: Now add tens. Add the next column to the left. This is the tens column. We are actually adding up tens: so 9 + 4 (= 13) is really 90 + 40 = 130. Write down 3, carry 1.

```
  9 2
+ 4 6
-----
? 3 8
1
```

The number carried over is really ten 10's (which we write as 100), so now the carried 1 goes into the hundreds column.

Step 4: There are no more columns of numbers to add above the line to the left, so the number carried over is placed, on its own, in the hundreds column.

   This makes the final answer 138.

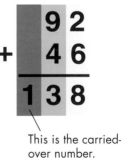

```
  9 2
+ 4 6
-----
1 3 8
```

This is the carried-over number.

Remember... Each column has a value: units, tens, hundreds. If adding a column gives an answer bigger than 9, you carry the left-hand number to the next column to the left, writing it down below that column so you don't forget it.

Word check

Three-digit number: A number between 100 and 999.

Two-digit number: A number between 10 and 99.

Adding several numbers

In many cases you have to add several numbers together.

Take these numbers, for example:

13 + 35 + 46 + 57 = ?

They are the numbers of coupons collected by each member of a club. The club leader needed to know the total because when the club had enough coupons, the local superstore would give them a new computer.

The club leader lined the numbers up in a long column to add them together.

First add the units column.
   To do this, either add from the top or the bottom. In this case we add from the top down.

100	10	1
	1	3
	3	5
	4	6
	5	7

We add the top two numbers in the right-hand column first:
3 + 5 = 8

Now add the next number to this total:
8 + 6 = 14

Now add the last number to this total:
14 + 7 = 21

Write 1 in the units column, carry 2 into the tens column.

	1	3
	3	5
	4	6
+	5	7
?	?	1
	2	21

The numbers in the units column add up to 21. The 1 unit is written in the units column, and the 2 representing 2 tens, or 20, is written below the tens column.

Next add the tens column.

To do this, either add from the top or the bottom. In this case we have decided to add from the bottom upward but you could, if you find it easier, add from the top.

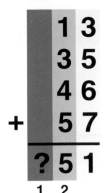

You can add the numbers in a column from top to bottom or bottom to top. See the Turn-Around Rule on page 19.

We add the bottom number to the number carried over:
5 + 2 = 7

Now add the next number to this total:
4 + 7 = 11

Now add the next number to this total:
3 + 11 = 14

Now add the top number to this total:
1 + 14 = 15

Write 5 in the tens column, carry 1 into the hundreds column.

Since there are no more hundreds to add, put 1 into the answer, which is 151.

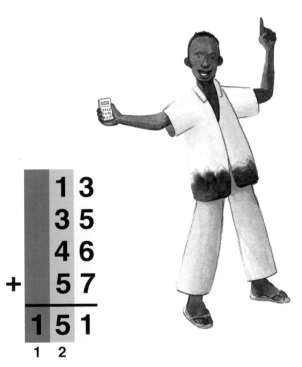

Remember... The longer the column of figures, the easier it is to make a mistake. So it is important to check the calculation. We do this by adding in the opposite order. In this way we add different numbers together and are less likely to repeat any mistake we might have made the first time.

Calculator check...

Electronic calculators are everywhere today. You should always work out single and two-digit additions in your head using the techniques shown in this book where possible. But for longer additions you may find a calculator useful.

Adding hundreds or thousands

A very big number, such as **645**, is six hundred (**600**) and (**+**) forty (**40**) (**+**) five (**5**). So it has three columns.

Adding large numbers is just as simple as adding smaller ones. You still simply organize your numbers into columns and carry to the left.

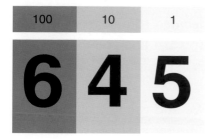

100	10	1
6	**4**	**5**

645 contains numbers in the hundreds column as well as numbers in the tens and units columns.

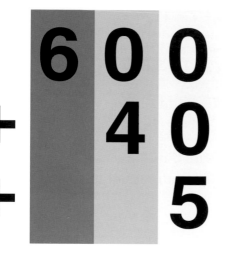

Charity raffle

The school had been planning a raffle to raise money for their favorite charities. They decided that there would be a competition between classes – everyone in the class that sold the most tickets would get a free burger lunch.

At the time of the raffle one class had sold 252 tickets, another class had sold 237 tickets, the third class had sold 216 tickets, but the fourth class had sold as many as 328 tickets.

While the winning class set off to get its free lunch, the head teacher found out how many tickets were actually sold.

This is what she found:

Step 1: Line up the numbers, then start with the units. In this case it is: 8 + 6 + 7 + 2 = 23, that is 20 + 3, so write down 3 in the units and carry 2 into the tens column.

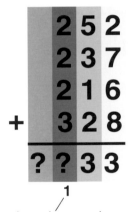

	1,000	100	10	1
		2	5	2
		2	3	7
		2	1	6
+		3	2	8
	?	?	?	3

This is the carried-over number of tens. **2**

Step 2: Now add the tens column. Start with the carried-over number: (2) + 2 + 1 + 3 + 5 = 13. Since we are adding tens, this is really 130. Write down 3, carry 1.

	2	5	2
	2	3	7
	2	1	6
+	3	2	8
?	?	3	3

This is the carried-over number of hundreds. **1**

Step 3: Add the hundreds column. Start with the carried-over number: (1) + 3 + 2 + 2 + 2 (= 10). Since we are adding hundreds, this is really 1,000.

   Write down 0 and carry 1. Since we have no more columns to the left, we put the 1 in the thousands column.

	2	5	2
	2	3	7
	2	1	6
+	3	2	8
1	0	3	3

This is the carried-over number of thousands. **1**

A total of **1,033** tickets has been sold.

Remember... If you have to add big numbers, you will need more columns to work in. In this example we needed to draw in a thousands column.

Adding numbers from distance charts

There are many ways of writing down numbers. In atlases it is common to see a distance chart looking like a triangle. To find the distance, you read the first place along the row and the second place up the column.

Distance charts allow you to work out how far your trip will be. But you will need to add each distance together to get the total distance of the trip.

Donald and Glenn were planning a journey across Canada with their parents.

They had bought a road map that included a distance chart. They needed to see how far they would travel in total.

Adding the distances

Here are the distances that Donald and Glenn got from the chart on the right.

Vancouver to Calgary 1,090 km
Calgary to Winnipeg 1,350 km
Winnipeg to Montreal 2,390 km
Montreal to Halifax 1,280 km

Now they had to add them up.

Check to see that you agree with them. Notice that the chart gives kilometers because Canada uses the metric system of measurement.

Distance in kilometers

	Halifax	Montreal	Saskatoon	Vancouver	Winnipeg
Calgary	5011	3750	626	1090	1350
Halifax		1280	4448	5995	3655
Montreal			3184	4731	2390
Saskatoon				1681	783
Vancouver					2330

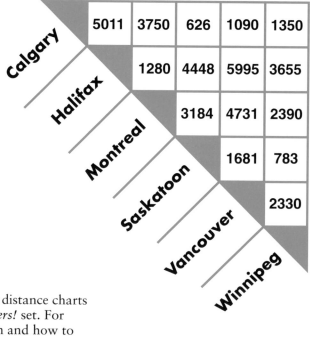

Book link... For more information on distance charts see the book *Charts* in the *Math Matters!* set. For more information on the metric system and how to convert between kilometers and miles see the book *Grids and Graphs* in the *Math Matters!* set.

Step 1: Put the numbers below each other in a column, lining them up to the right.

Add the right-hand column first. In this case it is: 0 + 0 + 0 + 0 = 0
So write down 0.

Add the next column to the left. This is the tens column. From the bottom up this is: 8 + 9 + 5 + 9 = 31

So write down 1, carry 3.

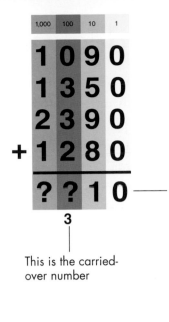

These numbers add to less than 10, and so there is nothing to carry over

This is the carried-over number

Step 2: Add the next column to the left. This is the hundreds column. First add the carried-over 3 to the bottom number:
3 + 2 + 3 + 3 + 0 = 11
So write down 1 and carry 1 to the next column left.

Step 3: Add the next column to the left. This is the thousands column. First add the carried-over 1 to the bottom number:
1 + 1 + 2 + 1 + 1 = 6
So write down 6.

This is the carried-over number

The total journey was 6,110 km – a journey of a lifetime!

Remember... 0's are place holders.
Notice that many distances end in 0. But you cannot ignore the 0 because it is part of the number. It is holding the place of no units. You must add 0's just like any other number.

Book link... For more on the use of 0's see the book *Numbers* in the *Math Matters!* set.

Adding decimal numbers

Decimals are numbers that combine whole numbers with parts of whole numbers, for example, **2.31**.

To separate numbers with a value of **1** or more from numbers less than **1**, a mathematical "period" is placed after the units so that we know which one it is. The period is called a decimal point.

Book link... For more information about decimals see the book *Decimals* in the *Math Matters!* set

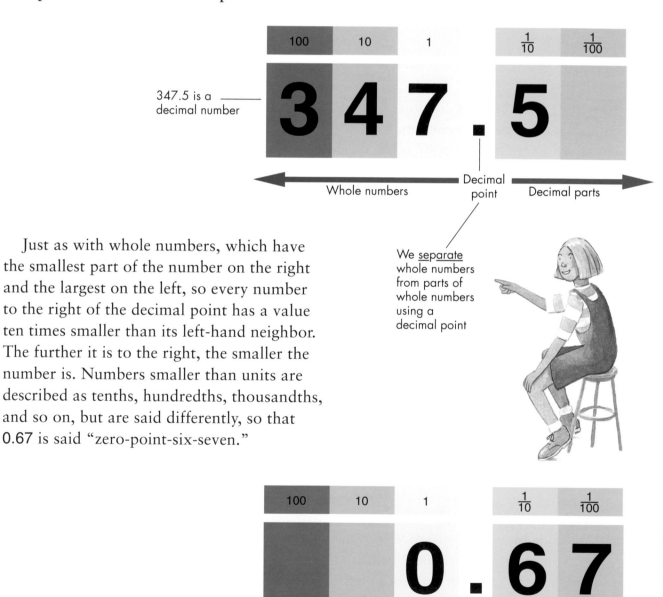

100 | 10 | 1 | $\frac{1}{10}$ | $\frac{1}{100}$

347.5 is a decimal number

3 4 7 . 5

Whole numbers — Decimal point — Decimal parts

We <u>separate</u> whole numbers from parts of whole numbers using a decimal point

Just as with whole numbers, which have the smallest part of the number on the right and the largest on the left, so every number to the right of the decimal point has a value ten times smaller than its left-hand neighbor. The further it is to the right, the smaller the number is. Numbers smaller than units are described as tenths, hundredths, thousandths, and so on, but are said differently, so that 0.67 is said "zero-point-six-seven."

100 | 10 | 1 | $\frac{1}{10}$ | $\frac{1}{100}$

0 . 6 7

Example: Add 347.5 and 26.67

Step 1: Place the numbers above each other, lining them up around the decimal point.

100	10	1	$\frac{1}{10}$	$\frac{1}{100}$
3	**4**	**7 .**	**5**	
+	**2**	**6 .**	**6**	**7**
?	**? ?**	**?**	**?**	

Step 2: If the numbers have an unequal number of decimals, write extra zeros to fill the columns. In this case a zero (0) has been written after the 347.5 to make it 347.50.

Write an extra 0 here

3	**4**	**7 .**	**5**	**0**
+	**2**	**6 .**	**6**	**7**
?	**? ?**	**?**	**?**	

Step 3: Start adding from the right as usual.

3	**4**	**7 .**	**5**	**0**
+	**2**	**6 .**	**6**	**7**
3	**7 4**	**1**	**7**	
	1	1		

Step 4: Put a decimal point in the answer exactly below the other decimal points. This gives the final answer.

3	**4**	**7 .**	**5**	**0**
+	**2**	**6 .**	**6**	**7**
3	**7 4 .**	**1**	**7**	
	1	1		

The decimal numbers lined up

Remember... To add decimal numbers, first line them up around the decimal point. Then add the decimal numbers just as you would add whole numbers, beginning on the right. At the end put a decimal point in the answer in line with the others.

Word check

Decimal number: A number that contains parts of units as well as whole units. The decimal point is used to separate the units from the parts of a unit.

Decimal point: A dot written after the units when a number contains parts of a unit as well as whole numbers.

Adding minus numbers

Sometimes you will see numbers with a minus sign in front of them like this: −5. These are called minus numbers.

Weather forecast

One everyday place to find minus numbers is on a thermometer. So, for example, on a very cold day the thermometer might read minus 20°C (−20°C) on the Celsius scale, which is minus 4°F (−4°F) on the Fahrenheit scale.

Here is an example using Celsius. Suppose a weather forecaster said that the temperature overnight could fall to −5°C, but that the next day it might be 19°C warmer. What would the temperature be then?

To find the answer, we have to add 19 to −5:

$$(-5) + 19 = ?$$

We can use a thermometer marked off to cover the range of temperatures we are interested in like the one shown on the right to show that −5°C plus 19°C equals 14°C:

$$(-5) + 19 = 14$$

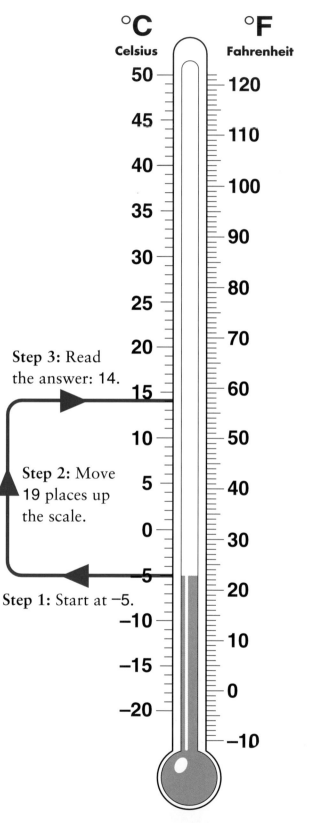

°C Celsius

°F Fahrenheit

Step 3: Read the answer: 14.

Step 2: Move 19 places up the scale.

Step 1: Start at −5.

Godiva and the chilling wind

Once upon a time in Coventry, England, there lived a beautiful lady called Godiva. Unfortunately, Godiva had to marry Earl Leofric, who was cruel to the people of Coventry.

Godiva wanted to help the townspeople and she pleaded with Leofric to lower the huge taxes he charged. But he would only agree if she would ride without clothes through the marketplace. Godiva asked the townspeople not to look as she rode through town. Then she mounted her white horse, wrapped her beautiful long blonde hair around herself, and rode through town. Leofric then had to lower the taxes.

Why might Godiva need to wrap herself up if no one was looking? Well, if, for example, the temperature had been 48°F, and it was a breezy day, the effect of the cooling breeze might have made it feel 9°F cooler. In that case the temperature would have felt like:

$$48 + (-9) = 39°F$$

Or in Celsius, if it was really 9°C, and the cooling breeze made the temperature feel 5°C cooler, the temperature would have felt like:

$$9 + (-5) = 4°C$$

Weather forecasters talk about adding on the wind chill factor. That means adding on −5°C, which is the same as lowering the temperature by 5°C.

Word check

− : Between two numbers the symbol means "subtract" or "minus." In front of one number it means the number is a minus number.

+ : Between two numbers this symbol means "plus" and is the symbol for adding. In front of one number it means that the number is a plus number.

Minus numbers: The numbers that fall below zero on a number line (scale). Minus numbers or zero cannot be used for counting, only for measuring things like temperature. Minus numbers are also called negative numbers.

Plus numbers: The numbers that fall above zero on a number line (scale). They are called this to separate them clearly from minus numbers. Plus numbers are also called positive numbers.

Book link... Find out more about minus and plus numbers in the book *Subtracting* in the *Math Matters!* set.

Adding fractions

A fraction is a piece of something. For example, if a cake is cut in half, we are splitting it into **2 pieces.**

If those two pieces are put side by side again, the 2 pieces make up, or add up to, the whole cake once more.

We write each half piece as a fraction like this:

$$\frac{1}{2}$$

and say it as "one-half."

Now we know that two halves make a whole:

$$\frac{1}{2} + \frac{1}{2} = 1$$

Notice that each fraction has the same number on the bottom. This means we can combine them:

$$\frac{1}{2} + \frac{1}{2} = \frac{2}{2} = 1$$

When the top and bottom are the same number (such as ²⁄₂), this makes a whole one.

So the rule is, if you have fractions with the same number at the bottom, you can add the tops of the fractions together.

Parts of a fraction:

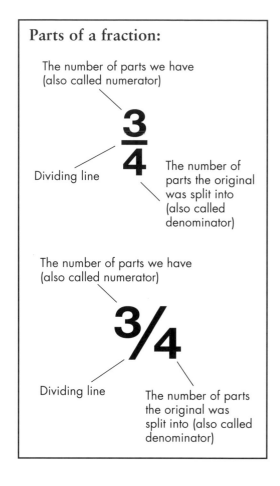

The number of parts we have (also called numerator)

$$\frac{3}{4}$$

Dividing line

The number of parts the original was split into (also called denominator)

The number of parts we have (also called numerator)

3/4

Dividing line

The number of parts the original was split into (also called denominator)

Adding fractions that are not similar

If we want to find the answer to this addition:

$$\frac{1}{3} + \frac{1}{4} = ?$$

First we need to make the fractions similar. We do this by multiplying the top and bottom of each fraction like this:

Multiply the top and bottom of ⅓ by 4. This makes ⁴/₁₂.

$$\frac{4}{12}$$

Multiply the top and bottom of ¼ by 3, This makes ³/₁₂.

$$\frac{3}{12}$$

Now we have two fractions with the same bottom number, and we can add them together.

$$\frac{4}{12} + \frac{3}{12} = \frac{7}{12}$$

Remember... To add fractions, the bottoms must be the same. If they are, just add the tops.

Book link... Find out much more about fractions in the book *Fractions* in the *Math Matters!* set.

Word check

Fraction: A special form of division using a numerator and denominator. The line between the two is called a dividing line.

Dividing Line: The line that separates the two number parts of a fraction. It is sometimes written horizontally — and sometimes sloping / .

Similar fractions: Fractions with the same denominator.

Adding to an equation

You have used equations throughout this book. They occur whenever you see an = sign. The idea is that the numbers on one side of an equals sign in an equation balance those on the other side.

For example: **12 + 13 = 25**

The word "equation" and the word "equals" both come from the same Latin word meaning level. You can see how this came about by thinking of the way that scales work. This diagram shows a pair of scales. On one side there are 4 cartons, and on the other side there are 2 bags.

So the scales show us the equation:

4 cartons = 2 bags

Let's shorten this to:

4c = 2b

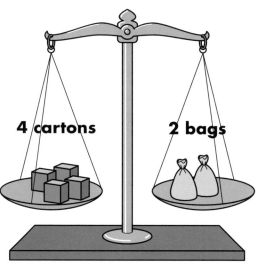

4 cartons   2 bags

Now, if we add 5 jars (5j) to the cartons, the scale pan with the jars and cartons will be heavier than the scale pan with the bags.

$$4c + 5j \neq 2b$$

Is not equal to

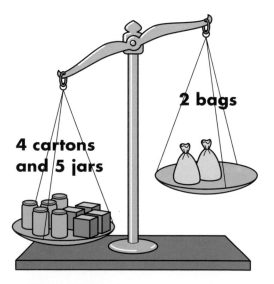

4 cartons and 5 jars   2 bags

To bring the scales back into balance again, you need to add the same amount to both sides, like this:

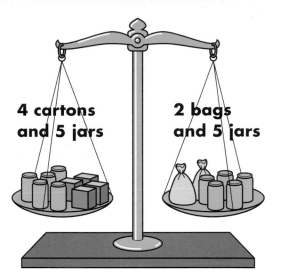

4 cartons and 5 jars — **2 bags and 5 jars**

Now the equation is balanced again:

$$4c + 5j = 2b + 5j$$

Finding unknowns

Knowing that an equation balances allows us to find an unknown number in questions like:

$$8 + \boxed{?} = 9 + 5$$

Here we need to know which number $\boxed{?}$ added to 8 will equal 9 + 5

From our adding facts we already know that 9 + 5 = 14

so:

$$8 + \boxed{?} = 14$$

By using our adding facts <u>backward</u>, we should also know that 8 + 6 = 14 So the unknown number is 6:

$$8 + 6 = 14$$

Notice that using adding facts backward is something we have not done before, but as you can see, it is very helpful.

Remember... If we do the same thing to both sides of an equation, it remains balanced.

Word check

= : The symbol for equals. We say it "equals" or "makes." It comes from a Latin word meaning "level" because weighing scales are level when the amounts on each side are equal.

≠ : The symbol for "is not equal to."

Equals: The things on either side of an equals sign are the same.

Book link... Find out more about equations, when to use addition and when to use subtraction in the book *Subtracting* in the *Math Matters!* set.

What symbols mean

Here is a list of the common math symbols together with an example of how they are used. You will find this list in each of the *Math Matters!* books, so that you can turn to any book if you want to look up the meaning of a symbol.

— Between two numbers this symbol means "subtract" or "minus." In front of one number it means the number is negative. In Latin *minus* means "less."

+ The symbol for adding. We say it "plus." In Latin *plus* means "more."

✕ The symbol for multiplying. We say it "multiplied by" or "times."

= The symbol for equals. We say it "equals" or "makes." It comes from a Latin word meaning "level" because weighing scales are level when the amounts on each side are equal.

$$(8 + 9 - 3) \times \frac{2}{5} = 5.6$$

( ) Parentheses. You do everything inside the parentheses first. Parentheses always occur in pairs.

—, /, and **÷** Three symbols for dividing. We say it "divided by." A pair of numbers above and below a / or — make a fraction, so ⅖ or $\frac{2}{5}$ is the fraction two-fifths.

■ This is a decimal point. It is a dot written after the units when a number contains parts of a unit as well as whole numbers. This is the decimal number five point six or five and six-tenths.

Glossary

Other symbols used in this book.

≠ : The symbol for "is not equal to."

Terms commonly used in this book.

Adding: A quick way of counting.

Adding facts: The numbers produced by adding together numbers that we use a lot, such as 3 + 4 = 7. These are facts we remember rather than work out each time.

Adding square: Simple adding facts arranged in a square pattern to make it easier to learn them.

Carrying: In adding or multiplying, when the working column total is bigger than 10, this is the method of adding the left digit at the bottom of the column on the left.

Counting: Finding the result in a set of things by giving each item a number one more than the last one used.

Decimal number: A number that contains parts of units as well as whole units. The decimal point is used to separate the units from the parts of a unit.

Decimal point: A dot written after the units when a number contains parts of a unit as well as whole numbers.

Digit: The numerals 1, 2, 3, 4, 5, 6, 7, 8, 9, or 0. Several may be used to stand for a larger number. They are called digits to make it clear that they are only part of a complete number. So we might say, "The second digit is 4," meaning the second numeral from the left. Or we might say, "That is a two-digit number," meaning that it has two numerals in it, tens and units.

Dividing Line: The line that separates the two number parts of a fraction. It is sometimes written horizontally — and sometimes sloping / . It is also called the division line. It is one of the signs mathematicians use for dividing. The other is ÷.

Equals: The things on either side of an equals sign are the same.

Equation: A number sentence using the = symbol, telling us that two different ways of writing a number are the same. For example, 2 + 2 = 4 and 9 − 5 = 4.

Fact family: A group of related facts about adding and subtracting or about multiplying and dividing.

Flat: A large square representing 100. It can also be made up of ten "longs" put side by side.

Fraction: A special form of division using a numerator and denominator. The line between the two is called a dividing line.

Long: A long shape representing 10.

Minus numbers: The numbers that fall below zero on a number line (scale). Minus numbers or zero cannot be used for counting, only for measuring things like temperature. Minus numbers are also called negative numbers.

Plus numbers: The numbers that fall above zero on a number line (scale). They are called this to separate them clearly from minus numbers. They are the same as counting numbers. Plus numbers are also called positive numbers.

Single-digit number: A number between 0 and 9.

Sum: The result of adding two or more numbers. *See* Total.

Three-digit number: A number between 100 and 999.

Total: The answer to an adding problem. *See* Sum.

Turn-Around Rule: When we add or multiply the same two numbers, the answer is the same no matter which of the numbers comes first (but it does not hold for subtracting or dividing).

Two-digit number: A number between 10 and 99.

Unit: 1 of something. A small square shape representing 1.

Set index